The Year of Release

Daily Manna

30-Day Prayer Journal

Maxine Y. Kershaw

Copyright © 2020 Maxine Y. Kershaw

All rights reserved. No part of this publication may be reproduced, distributed, or transmitted in any form or by any means, including photocopying, recording, or other electronic or mechanical methods, without the prior written permission of the publisher, except in the case of brief quotations embodied in critical reviews and certain other noncommercial uses permitted by copyright law. For permission requests, write to the publisher, addressed "Attention: Permissions Coordinator," at the address below.

ISBN: 978 -1 -7351479-7-1 (Paperback)
978 – 1-7341479-8-8 (E-book)

Library of Congress Control Number: 2020902953

Front cover image by Prize Publishing House, LLC
Book design by Prize Publishing House, LLC

Printed by Prize Publishing House, LLC in the United States of America.

First printing edition 2020.

Prize Publishing House
P.O. Box 9856
Chesapeake, VA 23321

www.PrizePublishingHouse.org

Because it is called the Lord's Release...

Deuteronomy 15:2b

Preface

Warning!!!

The Bible says to "pray without ceasing"; yet as believers we are set on "ceasing to pray". Not praying is equivalent to driving without headlights in the dark. Most headlights come on automatically unless, at some unsuspecting moment, they are turned off manually. Thus, there is an assumption that the light is on until other drivers start **flashing** to indicate **YOUR** lights are off!

This incredible prayer journal is a **headlight FLASH** indicator to turn the lights of prayer **ON** so that, through prayer, you are able to hit the bull's-eye as you pray, be spiritually awakened to specific areas to pray, and ignite a fire to return to the altar.

Acknowledgements

Like the song says, it's been a long time coming! Early one morning on a Spiritual Awakening call led by **Prophetess Barbara Calloway**, I could sense the presence of the Lord *"for real"* that it was time for release of this book. As she prayed and prophetically declared, "Someone on the line has unfinished books and things that were started but not finished; God is calling us to FINISH!" I got off the call and, within a few hours, was in touch with this amazing company, Prize Publishing House, and here we go! **Tiffany Thomas**…girl, there is a star in your crown in glory for your expertise, anointing and gifting to do what you do…Thanks ma'am!

I want to thank **all of the supporters** over the years for edging me along and touching my life at various times to keep going, and to keep ministering the way God has anointed and gifted me to minister and to write a book *(smile)*.

Mother Marcella Bristow, I remember the night you said, "You have too much to say, you need to write a book". Thank you!

To **my church family** and my baby – **Women of Strength (WOS)**, you have helped me stay true to course as the First Lady, Evangelist, sister and friend. Thank you!

"A New Word, A Known Word, A NOW Accountability" prophetically declared in Sunday School from my brother **Reginald "Reggie" Harris**! Sir, you have no idea the impact this declaration hovers over my life… Wow!

Evangelist Joyce Rogers, I will never forget the message "Restoration has Finally Come". It was my first glimpse of *transforming from a WOMAN with an issue to BEING made WHOLE!* A star added to your crown, sis. Thank you!

Evangelist Deborah Hollins-White, Evangelist Johnnie Evans, and Evangelist Hope Evans, thank you for giving me your ear and taking the time to talk me through matters.

Brax Brax, Zoe Zoe, Sydney, you LIGHT up my life!

To my husband, **Bishop Keith A. Kershaw**, I love you and appreciate all you bring to my life to make me a better me. **Rachel Victoria "Pookie"**, my greatest joy is YOU!

Contents

Day 1: Release our Fathers and Mothers (Spiritually and Naturally) 1
Day 2: Release Health (Spiritually and Naturally) 4
Day 3: Release of Being Controlled by the Lust of the Flesh, Lust of the Eyes and the Pride of Life 8
Day 4: Release from Backward to Forward 12
Day 5: Release Name Change to Character Change (Stop Letting the Devil Call You Out of Your Name!) 15
Day 6: Release to Believe…AGAIN! 19
Day 7: Release from Abnormal Hearing 22
Day 8: Release on Idolatry 26
Day 9: Release from the Spirit of Fear 29
Day 10: Release My Tongue from Speaking Guile 33
Day 11: Release to Change 37
Day 12: Release from Bondage in the Mind 41
Day 13: Release from Shame and Confusion 45
Day 14: Release, Sow, and Reap 49
Day 15: Release to Walk in Righteousness 53
Day 16: Release for Purpose 56
Day 17: Release from Being OVERWEIGHT 59
Day 18: Released to Increase 63
Day 19: Release Through an Indwelling Word and Prayer Life 66
Day 20: Release for Healthy Marriages 70

Day 21: Release for the Children 75
Day 22: Release for the Nations 78
Day 23: Release Among Pastors 81
Day 24: Release Among Pastor's Wives 86
Day 25: Release of Intercessors 89
Day 26: Release from Generational Curses 93
Day 27: Release from Infirmities 96
Day 28: Release from the Spirt of Offense 99
Day 29: Release from Adultery 104
Day 30: This is the Lord's Release 108

Day 1

Release our Fathers and Mothers (Spiritually and Naturally)

Scripture: *Matthew 18:27 – "Then the lord of that servant was moved with compassion, and loosed him, and forgave him the debt."*

Through the leading of the Holy Ghost, the Father led us to open the Women of Strength Prayer Line with "RELEASING" our fathers and mothers (spiritually and naturally). As you walk through your day, please guard your heart, mind, soul and body. To RELEASE means you are OPEN. You are open to RELEASE OUT, but you are also open to RECEIVE IN; be careful today as you open your WOUNDS so that you do not get an infection. Keep it open but recover from the infections of the devil.

God has given YOU the power to RELEASE your fathers and mothers. For WHATEVER the reason or cause of pain, they need your RELEASE (forgiveness).

Our fathers and mothers may have hurt us through lack of protection, by their words, not being attentive, not providing enough support, being absent, being poor parents, or not providing the direction you may have needed. Whatever the situation… RELEASE them today; not tomorrow, TODAY!

You say, "Lady Kershaw, it's not that easy" – that is the EXCUSE you have held on to far too long… LET IT GO! You will be empowered to do ministry (spiritually and naturally) as you release your fathers and mothers today. Finally, remember the Word from our spiritual father to be "Fused with the SWORD". Today we operate in the POWER of ONENESS and NOTHING shall be withheld from us.

Prayer

Father, in the name of Jesus, I come to you confessing unforgiveness I've held against my mother and father. I renounce the spirit of unforgiveness, and I declare it will no longer have any legal right to keep me from honoring my father and mother, which is the first commandment with promise. I decree and declare that the generational curse of unforgiveness is broken and it stops with me! I decree my children and my children's children will not be faced with abandonment of an absent parent, but both mother and father will be present and active in their lives to train them in the way that they should go, and it won't depart from them according to Proverbs 22:6. Amen.

Journal
The Lord's Release

Day 2

Release Health (Spiritually and Naturally)

Scripture: *3 John 1:2 – "Beloved, I wish above all things that thou mayest prosper and be in health, even as thy soul prospereth."*

I don't want to be worldly, wealthy and lose my soul. What would it profit a man to gain the whole world and lose his own soul? (Matthew 16:26).

I want to be led by the still waters where my soul can be restored. My soul is easily disquieted within me and I slip into an unhealthy place. Remember to decree and declare health over your soul (your mind, will and intellect). My natural and spiritual self should align in good health.

What does it take to be healthy? Proper diet, remaining in prayer and the Word, fellowship with the saints and fasting, to name a few spiritual staples. Lord help us to be conscious of being in good health not only at the beginning of the new year, but ALL year. Dwell in a wealthy-healthy place Women of Strength and Men of Valor!

3 John 1-4 – "The elder unto the well-beloved Gaius, whom I love IN THE TRUTH. Beloved, I wish above all things that thou mayest prosper and

BE IN HEALTH, EVEN as thou SOUL prospereth. For I rejoiced greatly, when the brethren came and testified of the TRUTH that is in thee, EVEN AS thou WALKEST IN THE TRUTH. I have no greater joy than to hear that my children WALK IN TRUTH."

The HOLY GHOST has ignited us to RELEASE health. So many sicknesses have crept in among us and are trying to set up permanent residence in the "temple of the Holy GHOST" (our physical bodies). At the same time, some of these same sicknesses and diseases are likewise manifesting in the spiritual. God has called us to "prosper and be in good health, EVEN AS our soul prospereth." We no longer abide in DENIAL regarding our physical or spiritual health. The enemy would rather we deal with SYMPTOMATIC deliverances than to get to the root of it. But today we take authority over every manner of sickness and disease in the natural and spiritual. I should be careful not to spiritualize every issue but should consider that arthritis has surely crept into our ministries and is constantly attacking the bones and joints for a crippling effect. However, God has called us to walk in TRUTH today about every manner of sickness and disease. We NO MORE abide in DENIAL!

Arthritis – crippling of joints and bones; back pain – core strength area; weight – up and down; poor appetite restrictions; lack of sleep – worry, anxiety and trust; high blood pressure; too much of something; this is a "trigger."

Cancer takes on many forms and has many different points of location and will SPREAD if not caught in time for treatment.

Bipolar Disorder – extreme; Lupus – body attacks itself. WHEW! Chromes Disease – form of Lupus – degenerative in nature; Extreme – itchy "ears"; Allergies – can easily get a "reaction" out of you; Diabetes – diet related; Weakness – lack of strength (anointed but weak); Tumors – growths; Excess heart trouble; WOW! Spots on the tongue/liver – indicator: Hepatitis; Foot problems – can't walk. WOW – you know!

The list goes on and on. Please cover yourself in the natural and spiritual TODAY. This is not an all-inclusive list, just a few. Study and see if God will give revelation to any sickness that may dwell in you. Be HEALED, BE DELIVERED and BE SET FREE!

Prayer

Father, in Jesus' name, we pray that You keep our bodies free of disease. Strengthen those that have been afflicted by illness or an attack of the enemy. Heal them and cause them to recover. Lord, You are the one that heals the broken hearted and binds up their wounds. So, we pray that You would heal according to Your will. Then God, help us to realize that our bodies are not our own; we are the temple of the Holy Ghost. Teach us to number our days that we may apply our hearts to wisdom. Help us begin to practice health and righteous living. I pray that we prosper and enjoy good health even as our souls prosper. I pray now against every would be distractive, destructive spirit, the spirit of mental illness, emotional struggles, feelings of hopelessness and abandonment the spirit of suicide and loneliness. Lord, help us to focus our minds on You that we may be kept in perfect peace; Your peace that passes all understanding that will keep our hearts and minds through Christ Jesus, Amen.

Journal
The Lord's Release

Day 3

Release of Being Controlled by the Lust of the Flesh, Lust of the Eyes and the Pride of Life

Scripture: *1 John 2:15-16 – "Love not the world, neither the things that are in the world. If any man loves the world, the love of the FATHER is NOT in him. For all that is in the world, the LUST of the FLESH, and the LUST of the EYES, and the PRIDE of LIFE, is not of the FATHER, but is of the world."*

Today, we release our fleshly driven appetites and our lustful driven desires and the "I" (pride) syndrome and are fully restored with our Father in Heaven who is qualified to show us how to govern the affairs of this life.

We ask our Father to restore ORDER to the places that have become disorganized to the point that we have been left to making the "best" decision for ourselves. God NEVER intended for us to be led through the flesh and He surely doesn't want us to lead ourselves. He created a people that would obey HIM. But the enemy has crept in and, rather than operating and functioning as a body, we are reduced to mere "body parts" all over the place. Families are being destroyed through the lust of the flesh and this is NOT alright with the FATHER.

We are in debt because we "SEE" things we can't afford, and the LUST of our eyes drives us to make a purchase that we can't afford. The "I" syndrome keeps us isolated from our spiritual family and glued to the pews when we should be and need to be operating in the ministry. We need to let GOD take the throne of our hearts. Pride caused Satan to fall far from GOD (literally).

Satan is using the same tactics to get you to fall away from your Father – through pride (that "I" syndrome). We need each other! Don't let your physical desires (lust of the flesh), personal desires (lust of the eyes) or self (I) (pride of life) cause you to stay disconnected. Resist the devil and he WILL flee from you. We ALL are tempted through our individual weakness, but we can all be RESTORED by allowing the Father to take FULL control of our BODY, MIND, SOUL and SPIRIT!

Prayer

1 John 2:16 – "For all that is in the world, the lust of the flesh, and the lust of the eyes, and the pride of life, is not of the Father, but is of the world."

Father, in the name of Jesus, we come against this spirit of lust that has attached to our flesh, lust in our eyes and our spirit of pride. We need You to bring our body into subjection according to Your Word from these ungodly lustful sins. Keep our eyes on You and in Your Word. Take away every lustful spirit from us, from things You never intended for us to have. We only desire those things You have for us according to Your will. Take our eyes off the things You didn't intend for us to have. We ask that You forgive us for wanting things that are not of Your will.

According to Your Word in Matthew 6:13, "And lead us not into temptation", Father, it is Your will that we enter not into temptation. Temptation is to entrap us to fall from Your grace. It is Your will for us not to fall into sin. You said in Your Word, "Yield not to temptation, for yielding is sin". 'Ole slew foot, we serve notice to you today, no longer will we allow you to dangle lustful things and people before us. We commit our eyes to the Lord; we see what He sees in Jesus' name. Father, we confess the Word of God over our life. You said in Your Word, "If any man be in Christ, he is a new creature." We're new because You have declared us new. No longer will we operate in the spirit of pride, where pride says it's okay to go against the will of God to purchase this or that, it's okay to want what we want and no longer will we operate under the spirit of Satan's lustful will. 'Ole slew foot is a fallen demon, why listen to him. Lord, You know what we need before we ask. Amen.

Journal
The Lord's Release

Day 4

RELEASE FROM BACKWARD TO FORWARD

Scripture: *Philippians 3:13-14 – "Brethren, I count not myself to have apprehended; but this ONE THING I do, FORGETTING those things which are BEHIND, and reaching FORTH unto those things which are BEFORE, I press toward the mark for the prize of the high calling of God in Christ Jesus."*

Today is a day of pressing FORWARD! Forget those hurts, pains, abuses, bad experiences, bad relationships…whatever! God has called us to move from that place of the "past" to our present and future. No longer will the things of old keep us so bound that we are not able to move to the next dimension in God. God is assuring you that He has "new" blessings in store for you. I keep hearing the Lord say, "stop rewinding", "press play". Play mode moves us forward, not backward!

We rebuke the enemy that would keep us tied to "old" stuff. No more rehearsing the past. Press play and let's move FORWARD into our NEW possessions. Move in your thoughts and deeds. The word encourages us in Philippians 4:8, "Finally my brethren whatsoever things are TRUE, whatsoever things are HONEST, whatsoever things are JUST, whatsoever things are PURE, whatsoever things are LOVELY, whatsoever things are of GOOD REPORT; if there be any virtue, and if there be any praise, thing on these things."

Simply put one foot in front of the other and move FORWARD!

Prayer

Isaiah 43:18-19 – "Remember not the former things, nor consider the things of old. Behold, I am doing a new thing; now it springs forth, do you not perceive it? I will make a way in the wilderness and rivers in the desert."

Psalm 32:8 – "I will instruct you and teach you in the way you should go; I will counsel you with my eye upon you."

Father, as we journey forward on this righteous path You have set before us, we leave behind the past hurts, loses, disappointments, bad relationships, shame, guilt, people who didn't mean us any good, bad experiences, habits, life that had us weighed and bounded, etc. You said in Your Word according to Luke 9:62, "No one who puts his hand to the plow and looks back is fit for the kingdom of God". Father, as we move forward there is no looking backwards. Looking backwards means we're not fit for the kingdom. As we position our hand on the gospel plow, we are placing our hands in Jesus' hand for Him to lead and guide us on this path journey. We look forward in Jesus' name!

Journal
The Lord's Release

Day 5

Release Name Change to Character Change (Stop Letting the Devil Call You Out of Your Name!)

Scripture: *Genesis 32:24-28 – "And Jacob was left alone and there wrestled a man with him until the breaking of the day. And when he saw that he prevailed not against him, he touched the hollow of his thigh; and the hallow Jacob's thigh was out of joint, as he wrestled with him. And he said, Let me go, for the day breaketh. And he said, I will not let thee go, except thou bless me. And he said unto him, What is thy name? And he said, Jacob. And he said, Thy name shall be called no more Jacob, but Israel: for as a prince hast thou power with God and with men, and hast prevailed."*

In the words our 2007 Conference Coordinator, "What a way to start the day!". God has called us to walk in our God-given destiny but many of us still struggle with where He has called us TO, because who we ARE doesn't seem to line up with where He has positioned us to BE. Jacob had this same struggle but after a "real" encounter with God, Jacob was released from being his "same old self" *(I've been this way all my life self, I can't help it, this is just who I am self)*, to Israel; that is, having POWER with God and MEN!

God wants to change your NAME today! He's calling you, not by your biological name, but by the character He has established in you from the foundation of the world.

Some of you have accepted the lie from the enemy that you have always been this way and have always done it this way. Well CHANGE is on the horizon for you. Accept the change today. Walk in your newfound RELEASE! NO MORE being bound to trickery, taking the easy way out, being on a milk diet (spiritually), being inoperative in ministry, procrastination, indecisiveness, having a quick-temperament, being distant, being excessive and the list goes on and on… this is a new day and we have wrestled with an angel and a NAME CHANGE is on the horizon for YOU.

As one prayed this morning, "It is sealed by the King" and when He decrees a thing, you are authorized to do what has been assigned by the King. Today, you are released to operate in your new character, at a higher call! Like Jacob, you don't have to prove it to others, they will soon come to know that you have been in the presence of God.

Don't try and evoke a change by the words you speak only. Let God work a work on your character today. I call forth the ministry gifting to the body of Christ and like that prostitute who waits on the street corner, you and I both know, that's not her real name. Go evangelize to those that want to remain the "Jacobs" of the world and challenge them to be RELEASED to operate with a new NAME which they are called by God. Enjoy your new land and your new name!

Prayer

Father, You spoke to Jacob in Genesis 35:10 saying, "Your name is Jacob, but you will no longer be called Jacob; your name will be Israel." I thank You for the application of the Word to my life, that my name and character will match. I am no longer "whatever you've been called" but I am who You say that I am. For You are creator of Heaven and earth, giver of life. You spoke by way of Your Holy Spirit in Jeremiah 29:11 saying, "You know the plans you have for me, plans to prosper me, and not to harm me, plans to give me hope, and a future." The name change to match my character change aligns with Your Word that I am no longer a thief, a manipulator, a trickster, a whatever I have been called. Thank You, Father, for aligning my name and my character to my promising future. I am a new creature in Christ: old things are passed away; behold all things are become new (2 Corinthians 5:17). Amen.

Journal
The Lord's Release

Day 6

Release to Believe…AGAIN!

Scripture: *Mark 9:23-24 – "Jesus said unto him, if thou canst BELIEVE, ALL things are possible to him that believeth. And straightway the father of the child cried out, and said with tears, Lord, I believe; help thou mine unbelief."*

"IF" is a big little word, isn't it? This story on the surface appears to be a display of the powerlessness of the disciples. The deliverance had become a point of discussion to those who had taken their dibs at why no REAL deliverance had taken place in the life of this young boy. Many reasons surface the scene: 1) The disciples did not have power; 2) The young boy had been this way since a child – longevity; 3) The list of symptoms displayed to confirm his struggle. It seemed to be everybody else's issue until Jesus asks the father, how long is it ago since this came unto him? And the father's response is limited to asking for Jesus to have compassion on him.

Compassion alone will not bring deliverance! Jesus went to the root of the matter and challenged the father to BELIEVE, ALL things are possible. And through confession, the father asked with tears for Jesus to help his unbelief.

We have grown weary in believing God for the supernatural. It seems that the longer we are in a situation, the more comfortable we become and relaxed about being delivered from it.

God is RELEASING us to believe HIM...again. This dimension of faith requires us not to hide among the crowd discussing the issues but fortifying in faith to cast the source out.

No more silent storms; no more hiding amongst the crowd; no more nursing issues over them – we need a release to believe that all things are possible. Move beyond repeating the same thing over and over again. Verse 29 says, "This kind can come forth by nothing, but by PRAYER and FASTING."

Prayer

Proverbs 13:12 – "Hope deferred taketh the heart sick but when the desire cometh, it is a tree of life."

Psalm 37:4 – "Delight thyself also in the Lord; and he shall give you the desires of thine heart."

Father, we thank You that we walk by faith and not by sight. So even though there are things we have been waiting on to come to pass that have not yet manifested, we thank You that a "Delay is not a Denial!" We thank You that You have spoken a promise to us that Your plans are to prosper us and to give us an expected end (Jeremiah 29:11). Right now, we Believe Again! We Expect Again! Your promises DO NOT Spoil!! With confidence according to Your Word, it's on the way. Thank You for a "reset" button in my faith to Believe Again! Thank You for praying for me, Jesus, as You did for Peter. Thank You for making intercession for me to the Father. You are the author and the finisher of my faith. I Believe Again. In Jesus' name.

Journal
The Lord's Release

RELEASE FROM ABNORMAL HEARING

Scripture: *Revelation 3:22 – "He that hath an ear, let him hear what the Spirit saith unto the church."*

Can you hear me NOW? That is the question! God has called us to be released from abnormal hearing. Many of us have become deaf to the voice of God. It appears hearing what the Spirit has to say has been solely left to "someone else."

Our ears have become 1) Clogged up/impacted; 2) Subject to gossip and whispers; 3) A means to receive information with no real intent to partake in change after having heard a WORD. Our ears are a channel to our faith. Faith influences our beliefs and our speech. Speech moves the heart and the hand of God.

We have become distracted and dizzy. People with hearing disorders struggle in the midst because they must make physical adjustments at times to be in position to hear, and by the time they get in position, the speaker is finished. Hard of hearing people talk loudly and their response might be off because their hearing acuity is off. A deaf person sounds different than a person with their hearing sense intact. If you are not careful, you will laugh because of the distortion of their communication skills. When hearing is lost at an early age (immaturity in the church) they are often characterized as being wild and undisciplined and that might be true because they are not able to hear the instruction of correction – Wow!

Our Father is calling us back to normal hearing. If you have ears, you should spend some time listening to what God has to say. No more itching ears open to gossip, bad advice, verbal abuse, words from men and women of God that have not heard a Word from God – no more! Do you understand that it is hard to praise God without hearing? Oh, that might explain why we struggle in praise and worship – hmmm!

Being a hearer of the Word should move us to be a doer of the Word. We thank God today for the sense of hearing. God's ears are open to the cry of the saints. He can hear you… always!

Prayer

Isaiah 55:11 – "So shall my word be that goes out from my mouth; it shall not return to me void, but it shall accomplish that which I please, and it shall proper in the thing whereto I sent it."

Father, no longer will we allow the enemy to come and steal the Word of God from our hearing. We silence the voice of the enemy in Jesus' name. No longer will we allow him to twist the Word of God, to make us believe God didn't really say what He has spoken. When we hear God's word of truth, we will embrace it and guard the word of truth. No longer will we allow the enemy to whisper in our ears, *did God say* when we clearly know what the Lord has spoken. We will guard our ear entrance from the enemy. To keep the enemy from whispering in our ears, we keep him under our feet. We BIND all the lies from the enemy and no longer will we allow him to speak doubt or push false narratives (destroy relationships); no longer will we allow him to plot schemes in our ears. Don't be fooled by the tactics of the enemy. Don't allow the enemy to get close to your ears. Amen.

Journal
The Lord's Release

Day 8

Release on Idolatry

Scripture: *Exodus 20:1-3 – "And God spoke these words, saying I am the LORD thy God, which have brought thee out of the land of the land of Egypt, out of the house of bondage. Thou shalt have no other gods before me."*

God calls us to a RELEASE of idol gods. He wants to be LORD in our lives and have full control over our heart. You might think because you have not erected a physical statue that this word might not apply; however, the LORD reveals to us, while we might not be worshipping physical statues in this day and time, we have become consumed and distracted by other things and controlled by other sources, thus our worship is divided.

We are consumed in our thoughts, emotions, time, work, families and other related duties that tire us to the point that we are not able to enter into the holy of holies. Even our dependence on medications and to be counseled constantly has increased in this last day. Please understand the Holy Ghost calls for us to make sure that we are not worshipping other gods in any form.

No more distractions from other sources that would take away from the God that has brought us out of bondage. Understand that no other source will ever satisfy you like a real and consistent God.

Prayer

Father, in Jesus' name, I renounce all working of idolatry and I pray that You break every chain that would keep me bound to it. Help me to set my affections on things above and not on things of the earth. Lord, don't let me go astray after anything that doesn't bring glory to You. Purge me from every working of idolatry and I shall be clean, wash me and fill me with Your Holy Spirit so I may be pure from worldly lust; that I might walk after the spirit and not after the flesh.

Your Word says that You are a jealous God and Your glory You won't share with another. So, Lord help me to not stray from You or be found guilty of ever putting anything before You. Help me to always bare in remembrance that you are the God that created heaven and earth, that the earth is Yours and all that dwell in it.

Now God, I thank You that I realize I live, move and have my being because of You. Thank You for Your spirit that is empowering me to flee idolatry to make You Lord in and over my life. Amen.

Journal
The Lord's Release

Day 9

RELEASE FROM THE SPIRIT OF FEAR

Scripture: *2 Timothy 1:7 – "For God hath not given us the spirit of fear; but of power, and of love, and of a sound mind."*

Symptoms: Phobias, nightmares, sickness, death, worry, excessive timidity, stress, psychological complexes and heart attacks as listed in *Strongman's His Name... What's His Game* by Drs. Jerry & Carol Roberson. When we say, "He is Lord", I hope your praise is going to God the Father and not the devil the father.

When we operate and are controlled by fear, we are being led by the devil, not God the Father, for He has not given us the spirit of fear. Fear is complex because sometimes the manifestation of a thing does not always show the spirit of fear as its source. Many gifts to the body of Christ remain seated on pews because of fear to participate and operate in ministry. The fear of rejection or rebuke stifles the call of God on your life. God has given the body of Christ pastors so that our ministry gifts can be checked and matured properly, so you should not be afraid to operate. Let the Pastor do his/her perfecting that concerns you. The spirit of fear tells you they already got someone to do it, and you're probably right but the problem is, the ministry/the Kingdom needs more than ONE! Women of Strength and Men of Valor, you are RELEASED from the spirit of fear today. You are FREE to walk in dominion over every creeping thing that has tried to invade your life, especially those of you who are tormented in your sleep through nightmares and other tormenting forms that invade your sleep. You are RELEASED through the power of the Holy Ghost to REST in the Lord your God who has assigned angels to keep watch over you while you sleep.

Your heart and mind have become a "playground" for the enemy and his friends (stress, worry, fatigue, depression, double mindedness, impure thoughts, paralysis, etc.). All of them come out to play in your sleep and thus instead of sweet dreams you entertain insomnia. The spirit of fear is behind those negative thoughts that invade your "wake" times too.

We RELEASE the spirit of fear from his assignment in your life from sending a threat, as did Jezebel, to cause you to be so afraid that you've moved to a cave to hide, or in the case of overhearing a negative word, as David overheard Goliath defying the name of the living God. The same threat that paralyzed Saul and his army, gave David the courage to become a "giant slayer!" All the enemy has to do is roar and we are so scared. We will leave our place of safety and run, only to find ourselves running into danger as opposed to running from danger as taught by Bishop Keith A. Kershaw.

No need to be afraid of the terror by day or night, God's got you, Women of Strength and Men of Valor. You are RELEASED to love again. Use your God-given authority to move mountains again and to have a SOUND mind.

Prayer

2 Timothy 1:7 – "God has not given us a spirit of fear, but of power, love, and of a sound mind."

Father, You have spoken to us in Your Word that WHATSOEVER we shall loose on earth shall be loosed in heaven. Right now, in the name of Jesus, we take authority over the spirit of fear (False Evidence Appearing Real)! Spirit of fear be bound in Jesus' name! We confess that we are made perfect in love as perfect love casts out all fear (Galatians 5:13). Therefore, I am free to do what I've been called and chosen to do, in Jesus' name!

Journal
The Lord's Release

Day 10

RELEASE MY TONGUE FROM SPEAKING GUILE

Scripture: *1 Peter 3:10 – "For He that will love life, and see good days, let him refrain his tongue from evil, and his lips that they speak no guile."*

James 3:10 – "Out of the same mouth proceedeth blessing and cursing. My brethren, these things ought not so to be."

Guile – the ability to deceive or trick someone; sly, cunning intelligence.

Women of Strength and Men of Valor, in case you didn't know, what you SAY matters! Not only what you say but how you say it. One aspect we easily overlook, is the INTENT of what we say.

In the beginning God spoke and it was so, and He has given His children authority to operate in the earth with that same power. We are snared by the words of our mouths and our productivity and destiny are held captive because guile is found in our lips. We must mature to a place in God that we have the discipline to speak the right words over our situation and to each other.

Evil communication, guile, cursing, offense, bitterness and lack of faith continue to come out of our mouth or slip out because the intent is already in our heart. Out of the abundance of the heart the mouth speaketh.

The heart is desperately wicked, who can know it? So, if we have a mouth issue, it might be that we need a heart transplant. Don't live on the extreme and let the devil get you to say, "Nothing at all". No, let's just always speak the right things. Become an "I willer"; that is, I will BLESS the Lord at ALL times.

God is concerned about what we are allowing to proceed out of our mouth. He has RELEASED us today from speaking guile. A guard is set before our mouths to keep our tongue bridled from any form of evil communication.

Do you sometimes feel tied down and unable to break free? It might be that your bondage is in your mouth just as much as your freedom is. We spend too much time speaking negatively. It is disguised under the pretense of merely having to say it and get it off our chest – NO!

Saints operate in discipline. While the tongue cannot be tamed, it can be subject to the Holy Ghost.

As we are filled with the Holy Ghost, what is the initial sign? To speak with other tongues – WOW! When there is an inward work of Christ, there will be a change in your tongue. If you are having difficulty with your tongue speaking guile, seek the Lord to be filled with the Holy Ghost. You will find a new language in your mouth.

Prayer

Psalm 19:14 – "Let the words of my mouth and the meditation of my heart be acceptable in thy sight oh Lord, my strength and my redeemer!"

My God, my God! Please God, keep my tongue – the fires that started with my tongue speaking guile. The tongue as a "crouching tiger" releasing into the atmosphere death more than speaking life in the form of a joke, sarcasm, cynicism, silence (saying it without saying it), slips, fake apologies, and white, light blue, pink, or black lies…still guile.

"The tongue – a little member, and boasteth great things, Behold, how great a matter a little fire kindleth!" (James 3:5). Tame my tongue to bless and not curse. Words are seeds. Small seeds take root and grow into big trees and harvests. Be careful with your words as it might kindle a wildfire. God, You created an entire world with Your words! We are created in Your image and must be careful that we are not creating and destroying with our words. The Bible says, "Out of the same mouth come proceeded blessing and cursing" (James 3:10). My brethren, these things should not be so. LISTEN!

Jesus, help me to not offend or destroy with my tongue, but help me to be wise enough to restrain my lips lest I fall into transgression. Lord, I pray that Your spirit would lead me into all truth that I might have good success, and long life by keeping my tongue from evil and my lips from speaking deceit. Lord, I pray that You take away everything that is not like You; cleanse my hands and purify my heart. For the heart is deceitfully wicked and out of the abundance of the heart the mouth speaketh. So, search me oh God, know my heart, try me and know my thoughts, see if there be any wicked way in me. Then sanctify me, oh Lord, so that I will live my life in a way that would be honorable in Your sight. Amen.

Journal
The Lord's Release

Day 11

Release to Change

Scripture: *Ecclesiastes 3:1-8 – "To every thing there is a season, and a time to every purpose under the heaven: A time to be born, and a time to die; a time to plant, and a time to pluck up that which is planted; A time to kill, and a time to heal; a time to break down, and a time to build up; A time to weep, and a time to laugh; a time to mourn, and a time to dance; A time to cast away stones, and a time to gather stones together; a time to embrace, and a time to refrain from embracing; A time to get, and a time to lose; a time to keep, and a time to cast away; A time to rend, and a time to sew; a time to keep silence, and a time to speak; A time to love, and a time to hate; a time of war, and a time of peace."*

Reinhold Niebuhr wrote this prayer many years ago, "God grant us the serenity to accept the things we cannot change, courage to change the things I can and wisdom to know the difference".

Change is difficult for some. God has dispatched a season of change to the Women of Strength and Men of Valor. It seems as though the saints are not open to change but would rather embrace the most comfortable place and take the least path of resistance. In this lifetime, change is inevitable. The Father in heaven designed the world around things changing. Each morning we receive NEW mercies.

Be careful that you do not become complacent or stuck in one season of your life. If you have been in one season for seemingly an extended period of time, it's time now for you to be RELEASED to change. You ask, how? – through 1) Acceptance of the things you cannot change; 2) Having the courage to change the things you can; 3) Asking God for daily wisdom to know the difference.

The Word says all things work together for the good, the bad and the ugly. We are in a movement that we rebuke all that we perceive as negative and only accept or receive the aspects of our lives that seem positive. News Flash: GOD IS IN CONTROL of it ALL!

Be reminded that nothing escapes the eye of the all-seeing God. He will hasten to perform His Word in your life. Don't be afraid to embrace "new". Some may see the new land only filled with giants, but I thank God for the spy that will seek out the land flowing with milk and honey and, in spite of the giants, are willing to yet go in and possess the land.

Stop letting the enemy whisper that things will be this way always – that is not the truth. The truth is, "To everything there is a season (cycle/change) and a time to every purpose under the heaven" (Ecclesiastes 3:1).

 Prayer

Father, from the very beginning You brought about change, You created the heavens and the earth to a place that was void and surrounded by darkness. Even in death You bring about change. For Your Word says that we shall not sleep, but we shall all be changed in a moment, in the twinkling of an eye, at the last trumpet! Lord, I pray that I embrace change in my life because change is often evidence of You working for my good. Lord, I pray that You help me change the things in my life that keep me attached to the world. I pray for change in my life because I do not want to be conformed to this world. Instead, I need to be transformed by the renewing of my mind – that by trials and testing I may discern what is the will of You, what is good and acceptable and perfect. I pray for a change/renewal of my mind so that I may see a manifestation of change in the atmosphere around me. In Jesus' name.

Journal
The Lord's Release

Day 12

RELEASE FROM BONDAGE IN THE MIND

Scripture: *2 Corinthians 10:3-6 – "For though we walk in the flesh, we do not war after the flesh: (For the weapons of our warfare are not carnal, but mighty through God to the pulling down of strong holds;) Casting down imaginations, and every high thing that exalteth itself against the knowledge of God, and bringing into captivity every thought to the obedience of Christ; And having in a readiness to revenge all disobedience, when your obedience is fulfilled."*

We have walked in great victory today by RELEASING the bondage of the mind. The enemy has infiltrated the minds of the people of God causing our body to be at war with each other when God has called us to operate and function as many members but one body.

In the words of our founder, Charles Harrison Mason, today we "cast the devil out of the mind!" No more suspicion, doubt, wondering, idle, passive, judgmental, critical, anxious, confused or double minds will be a stronghold in the lives of the Women of Strength and Men of Valor. Our prayer today is that we will cast down every imagination that exalteth itself against the knowledge of God.

Watch your entry points (eyes, mouth, ears, hands, and nose). You absolutely, positively cannot watch shows and movies that stimulate your mind to go contrary to God's will, speak negatively, listen to the counsel of the ungodly (to include music that feeds your spirit and results in your mind being tied up in bondage – you want to watch your connections), nor inhale being surrounded by negativity. Through the Holy Ghost, I RELEASE over you the Word of God found in verse 6 that you would have a readiness to revenge ALL disobedience.

Don't let your tongue and emotions get in on the "thought" and before you know it a stronghold is set up in your mind or against someone else through offense.

Plead the blood of Jesus over your mind daily. Don't just empty your mind, for the enemy will find it an attractive place to build a new playground for himself and his friends (depression, anxiety, insomnia, offense, confusion to name a few). So, think on things that are true, honest, pure and just.

Fill your mind with the thoughts of God by reading His Word, memorizing His Word, speaking/rehearsing His Word in your daily conversations and PRAYING His Word. Joyce Meyer is one of my favorite authors. She has written a powerful book called *Battlefield of the Mind*. It is an awesome tool to have to help govern your Christian walk. Freedom in the mind is a wonderful thought.

Prayer

Heavenly Father, open our eyes to hear Your voice so clear and the strangers we won't follow. Empower us to shut out every voice that would bombard our minds causing us to do things not pleasing to You. Open our minds that we are able to think sound thoughts. Give us power to think on those things that are true, honest, just, pure, lovely and are of a good report. Help us to transform our thinking through Your Word and let this mind be in us that was also in Christ Jesus. We pray for the power to abhor that which is evil and cleave to that which is good. Then let the peace of God which passes all understanding guard our hearts and minds forever. We thank You now; for the plans You have for us – plans to prosper us and not to harm us, plans to give us hope and a future. Amen.

Journal
The Lord's Release

Day 13

Release from Shame and Confusion

Scripture: *Isaiah 61:7 – "For your SHAME ye shall have DOUBLE; and for CONFUSION they shall rejoice in their portion; therefore, in their land they shall POSSESS the DOUBLE: everlasting joy shall be unto them."*

This is a word to the remnant, not the masses. Everybody is walking around talking about they are blessed, and generally speaking they are. But those that POSSESS the DOUBLE are those that have endured the great shame and confusion that has been assigned to them, even from childhood, to be able to inherit the DOUBLE.

Why me Lord? Why my family? Why my house? Why my husband? Why my wife? Why my job? Why my finances? Why my children? Why my health? Why my church? Why my pastor? Why my mom and dad? Why???

From the foundation of the world, I purposed to bless my people and they will be blessed and have been blessed. But I have reserved for myself, a remnant, which I have called and chosen to myself to endure shame and confusion. Through the sifting and shifting that only "shame and confusion" could bring, these are positioned to receive DOUBLE!

As Lord of Lords, He endured the cross while they mocked Him, scorned Him, humiliated Him, beat Him, spat on Him, laughed at Him, passed judgment on Him…CRUCIFIED HIM. It didn't seem fair and the disciples were ashamed and embarrassed. I'm sure that they had dedicated their lives to follow our Lord and Savior. He was not able to deliver Himself. Through the shame of the cross, He stayed there because He understood a greater prize was in store for those who had gone on before believing Him, those looking on His shame believing Him and YOU, Women of Strength and Men of Valor, would believe Him through your shame and confusion.

Today is a day of strategic positioning for those who have stayed the course through the shame and embarrassment of the things you had to suffer. The confusion that arose as a result of your decision to follow a PROMISE only you could see. And even when your eyes were blinded by "Why me Lord", you somehow bounced back because you knew that God was too just to make a mistake. And even though you couldn't explain it, didn't like it, segregated, isolated, felt misunderstood, felt forsaken, suffered lack, felt cut off and disgraced…God's grace KEPT you in reserve for a day, THIS DAY, for you to POSSESS the DOUBLE!

In the words of an 'ole timely gospel – *put your time in, payday is coming after while* – It's PAYDAY! It's time to POSSESS the DOUBLE!

Prayer

Father, fill me with Your Word! Every Word spoken according to Your will, will not return void. I pray that You give me power to resist the dart of the enemy that reminds me of things that are in my past and I am overcome with shame. The shame that is a result of something someone else did that brings me to a place that makes me walk with a bowed down head and a heavy heart, please lift this burden off of me. Help me, oh Lord, to remember that You are a forgiving God. I ask You for forgiveness for the times I leaned to my own understanding in dealing with my shame. I ran into isolation. I need You Lord to keep my mind in perfect peace concerning those matters that are too difficult and overwhelming – that leads me down the path of guilt and shame. Help me to remember the people You have put in my life that will speak life and truth to me when I crave the pit of shame. I declare according to thy Word in Psalm 3:3, "But You, oh Lord, are a shield for me, my glory and the lifter up of mine head." Women of God, Men of Valor – "Lift up your heads, O ye gates, and be ye lift up, ye everlasting doors, and the King of glory shall come in…Who is the King of glory? The LORD of hosts, he is the King of glory" (Psalm 24:7-10). In Jesus' name.

Journal
The Lord's Release

Day 14

RELEASE, SOW, AND REAP

Scripture: *2 Corinthians 9:6 – "But this I say, He which soweth sparingly shall reap also sparingly; and he which soweth bountifully shall reap also bountifully."*

Proverbs 11:18 – "The wicked worketh a deceitful work: but to him that soweth righteousness shall be a sure reward."

One of my favorite shows is "Law and Order". Our RELEASE today sheds great understanding of law and order in regard to sowing and reaping. We are accustomed to sowing, sowing, sowing and then finally reaping. But God, that's enough right there isn't it? But God has RELEASED in intercession today that whatever we sow, we shall reap.

We do away with fainting and being dizzy about spiritual work. It is especially comforting to know that the law and order of sowing and reaping is defined in "whatsoever" terms. Whatsoever means an apple seed sown will produce apples for reaping. However, in the spiritual, a word sown will produce word. It might be difficult to see in the spirit if you limited the law of sowing and reaping to finances.

Like the children of Israel sat under the word, counsel and direction of their pastor, Moses, the Bible declares that many of them were overthrown in the wilderness. This implies that while many of them were overthrown, all of them were not overthrown. This word comes to transition you from being overthrown in the wilderness to REAP even while you're in your wilderness and until you get through the wilderness. We will see the results of the prayers prayed, the songs sung, and the word preached. Our ears and eyes will be open to hear and see the results of the seeds sown. The Lord will rebuke the devourer for His name sake off of our seeds. This word through prayer seeks for good soil!

Due season is not limited to calendar days and times. Due season has the same connotation as "now", "today", "granted", "suddenly", "immediately", "approved", and "in the same season". In due season, you SOW and REAP in the SAME season!

His word will search the earth to and fro seeking for the places that you have watered and planted so that God can bring the increase before it is returned VOID. I just heard the Lord say, "Increase is hand delivered by Him".

Law and Order: You are positioned to reap where you have sown!

Prayer

Lord, help me to plant what I want to grow! Seeds have been sown and the harvest testifies that all seeds were not good seeds. Roots have formed from seeds planted intentionally and unintentionally. I confess that I am in a mess and I need Your help, God, to be mindful of the seeds that flow out of my mouth. Your Word declares that the power of life and death are in the tongue (Proverbs 18:21). Heal me from "runaway" words – every vow I made with little regard to keeping it, unauthorized connections to things and people. A principle in the Word of God lets us know when you **sow** to the **spirit**, when you make **spiritual** investments by depositing the word of God (good **seed**) into your heart, you will harvest "life everlasting". It is a **spiritual** law of **sowing** and harvesting. So, God, "Let the words of my mouth and the meditation of my heart be acceptable in thy sight, oh Lord my strength and my redeemer" (Psalm 19:14). Amen.

Journal
The Lord's Release

Day 15

RELEASE TO WALK IN RIGHTEOUSNESS

Scripture: *Isaiah 64:6 – "Hallelujah, I'm declared righteous! All my righteousness is as filthy rags."*

Romans 3:10 – "As it is written, there is none righteous, no, not one."

There is nothing we could do to merit righteousness. I recognize Women of Strength and Men of Valor that righteousness is God's to declare over our lives. He justifies us. Glory! Imperfect, but He withholds no good thing from us according to Psalm 84:11.

This is powerful because you will be able to enjoy the fruit of YOUR own labor. In other words, no need to worry that someone else will reap the harvest of your sowing in the word day and night.

All of IT (whatever your IT is) is working together for YOUR good. In prayer, we are diligent in our verbal praise and worship, but there is also a time to listen – as I was challenged to do at one point. It was at that point that God could reveal His purpose to me about us, the Women of Strength and Men of Valor. As the woman of God led the prayer, the Lord showed me He will NEVER abandon HIS PURPOSE.

We are approaching the end of a scheduled time of prayer and fellowship. I'm sure the Lord will give us directions on how to continue at this level; however, He is calling us to a daily diet with Him that far supersedes our morning prayer time. He is offering, in exchange, a life of walking daily in righteousness with Him. "The Lord knoweth the way of the righteous" (Psalm 1:6).

For the Word of the Lord declares "Know ye not, that to whom ye yield yourselves servants to obey, his servants ye are to whom ye obey; whether of sin unto death, or of obedience unto righteousness" (Romans 6:16).

Prayer

For the Word of the Lord declares, "Know ye not, that to whom ye yield yourselves servants to obey, his servants ye are to whom ye obey; whether of sin unto death, or of obedience unto righteousness". Father, in the name of Jesus, I ask that you help us pursue righteousness, godliness, faith, love, patience, and meekness. Help us, Lord God, not to stumble in many ways, but to walk as a perfect man able to bridle our whole body according to James 3:2. As Your Word declares, even as we do so, Lord, we will be able to prove that which is the good, acceptable, and perfect will of God each and every day. In Jesus' name I pray. Amen.

Journal
The Lord's Release

Day 16

RELEASE FOR PURPOSE

Scripture: *Romans 8:28 – "And we know that all things work together for good to them that love God, to them who are the called according to his purpose."*

Each ingredient is just as important as the last product. In the case of baking a cake, no matter what the quantity is, or how much is put in, the quality is affected if the directions are not followed exactly. The claim "I did everything I was supposed to" is no longer sufficient. You see, if you are not brought to the end result, something was not done, overlooked or excused. Awake O Zion, put on strength as I worship comparatively with you, Women of Strength and Men of Valor.

The verse of Romans 8:28 continues to ignite my spirit man as the woman of God (K. Brown) escorted us into the presence of God. His revealed PURPOSE began to flow through the words she prayed, "It was me all along, I didn't intend for you to die, purposed by design, it was you all along!" Wherever you are at this very moment in time, in your purpose, you are NOT at your final destination! Please don't mistake that where you are currently is your PROMISED LAND! You are in view of it, but you haven't reached it YET! It doesn't matter who the "players" are, His purpose CANNOT be overthrown. He reminded me that what you sow and where you sow will be the exact place you will receive the HARVEST!

"All things are working together" is a powerful combination for a lover of God. God has RELEASED us with PURPOSE in mind. Enjoy every moment of your RELEASE! Don't be afraid to possess the new land because you see GIANTS. In the words of Donald Lawrence, giants FALL! God has purposed from the very beginning of time to bring you into perfect relationship with Himself; and for some of us, the route of the wilderness is the BEST route. He designed YOUR wilderness on PURPOSE!

Prayer

"For I know the thoughts that I think toward you, saith the LORD, thoughts of peace, and not of evil, to give you an expected end" (Jeremiah 29:11). Your thoughts toward ME are good and not evil and You want to give me my expected end! Thank you, Lord, for establishing purpose IN me. Thank you, Lord, that Your thoughts are not my thoughts, neither are Your ways my ways, saith the LORD (Isaiah 55:8). Leading and releasing me through my purpose driven life may take alternate routes, bypasses, backroads, mountains and valleys. Help me to remember in all my ways to acknowledge You and You promise to direct my path according to Proverbs 3:6. Deuteronomy 8:2 says, "And thou shalt remember all the way which the LORD thy God led thee these forty years in the wilderness, to humble thee, and to prove thee, to know what was in thine heart, whether thou wouldest keep his commandments, or no." Thank you that Your Word is a lamp unto my feet and a light unto my path (Psalm 119:105). Your Word gives me blessed assurance that You have released me on purpose. In Jesus' name.

Journal
The Lord's Release

Day 17

Release from Being Overweight

Scripture: *Hebrews 12:1 – "Wherefore seeing we also are compassed about with so great a cloud of witnesses, let us lay aside every weight, and the sin which doth so easily beset us, and let us run with patience the race that is set before us."*

I know it's a sensitive issue, but God cares about our TOTAL self, both naturally and spiritually. The number one killer/cause of death is mostly related to obesity. It's a sensitive issue, but it is an area the Holy Ghost wants to deal with today. Some may boast that you are not "physically" overweight, but you are "spiritually" overweight (existing off a milk diet when you should be eating and DIGESTING the meat of the Word). And some simply need a balance in their diet.

There are many excuses that come to mind why we eat so much. The sad part is, we control what we INTAKE. I use the word intake because some are overweight in their emotions by the things that they have become addicted to that causes excess worry, anxiety and stress. The goal is to run the race with patience. Patience is a very important word for a dieter (both physically and spiritually) because it puts in perspective that weight loss doesn't happen overnight, but with discipline, balanced diet and exercise, the goal will be achieved. Be careful of triggers (these increase your urge for something else). They are usually hidden and might not be easily detected. You might notice every time you eat that one thing, you always want something else. Or, it might be that after you commune with a particular person or activity, you have an obsessive urge for something ese.

An emotional eater needs to submit to the Word of God, as well as who you spend your time with that might stimulate your appetites. Pay attention by keeping a diary. Write the vision and it shall be made plain for you to RUN and read!

Have you plateaued in your efforts to lose weight both physically and spiritually? Then you must do something different in your exercise routine or diet. The Word encourages us to meditate on the Word both day and night. Are you getting enough Word in your diet? The Word says in everything give thanks. Are you being thankful enough? Are you lifting up your hands in the sanctuary on the regular or just when you feel like it?

No more FAD dieting! There is no one thing that will cure everything related to our excess weight gain, physically or spiritually. We need the Word, prayer, fasting and fellowship to maintain a good diet. Eat more FRUIT of the spirit (love, peace, longsuffering, gentleness, goodness, faith, meekness and temperance). It's low in calories and is good for you.

Prayer

Hebrews 12:1 declares "Wherefore seeing we also are compassed about with so great a cloud of witnesses, let us lay aside every weight, and the sin which doth so easily beset us, and let us run with patience the race that is set before us". Father, in the name of Your Son Jesus, I come to You about my being overweight – physically. Your Word says to confess my faults and I can be healed (James 5:16). I confess that I've overindulged, operated in a spirit of greed, developed an appetite and craving for more than I need, and have become comfortable with carrying the load. I've become desensitized to knowing when I've had enough. In this area, I've allowed flesh to be "lord". Wow! I confess that I am (*put in how many pounds*) overweight. and I know that faith without works is dead (James 2:14). So today, I ask You LORD to take Your rightful place in my heart. Conviction of the Holy Spirit, reside in my heart and mouth so that I may discipline my fleshly appetites and so that I may conquer this battle with my weight. I renounce every gate that leads me to eat more than I need or when I need it. Food is no longer my source but a resource to sustain life. I eat to live, not live to eat! I confess my sin to overindulge. I make a conscious decision that food will no longer have dominion over me. In Jesus' name.

Journal
The Lord's Release

Day 18

Released to Increase

Scripture: *Genesis 1:11-12 – "And God said, Let the earth bring forth grass, the herb yielding seed, and the fruit tree yielding fruit after his kind, whose seed is in itself, upon the earth, and it was so."*

And the earth brought forth grass, and herb yielding seed after his kind, and the tree yielding fruit, whose seed was in itself, after his kind; and God saw that it was good. Yielding seed, yielding fruit after his kind, whose seed is in ITSELF. This is a powerful sentence but to state this sentence in one word, it would be INCREASE!

Each seed should bring forth after its own KIND. We abide in INCREASE today, remaining steadfast and unmovable, always abounding in the work of the Lord for our labor is not in vain in the Lord (1 Corinthians 15:58). The work that you do for God will bring forth INCREASE. We shift to move in God that we will identify and recognize seed after His (our) kind. Who are you in the Kingdom of God? There are many other "who's" out in the earth just waiting to be linked up with its kind. Share the Word of God as He has commissioned us to seek out your kind also. You have come in contact with people, you have a knowing that you should share the gospel with them and there is a "likeness" about them that you just can't put your finger on. It might be that you have come face to face with a ministry link.

Our daughter looks like us; she has mannerisms like us because she is who we look like "together"!

Our increase is linked to our commission to share and link up with our own kind. Worshippers know worshippers, singers know singers, preachers know preachers, youth leaders know youth leaders, etc.

Do you see yourself in anyone, spiritually speaking? God created us in His IMAGE. And when HE returns, HE will be searching out those that look like HIM (after His kind).

One plants, one waters, but God gives the INCREASE.

Prayer

Jabez cried out to God of Israel, "OH, THAT YOU WOULD BLESS ME AND ENLARGE MY TERRITORY! LET YOUR HAND BE WITH ME AND KEEP ME FROM HARM SO THAT I WILL BE FREE FROM PAIN!" And God granted his request! Glory to God!! Father, I thank You for increase! Increase over every aspect of my life; my coming in and going out – Increase! An increase in wisdom, knowledge, understanding and the ways of the Kingdom. Open thou mine eyes that I may see the ways of the wicked plots and plans to intercept my increase. Enlarge our ministries that we will do greater works as we follow the leading of the Holy Spirit. We abide in Your Word that whatsoever we ask in Your name, YOU will do! We thank You for increase in our land and declare every place that the sole of our feet shall touch brings increase to us. In Jesus' name.

Journal
The Lord's Release

Day 19

Release Through an Indwelling Word and Prayer Life

Scripture: *Colossians 3:12-17 – "Put on therefore, as the elect of God, holy and beloved, bowels of mercies, kindness, humbleness of mind, meekness, longsuffering; Forbearing one another, and forgiving one another, if any man have a quarrel against any: even as Christ forgave you, so also do ye. And above all these things put on charity, which is the bond of perfectness. And let the peace of God rule in your hearts, to the which also ye are called in one body; and be ye thankful. Let the word of Christ dwell in you richly in all wisdom; teaching and admonishing one another in psalms and hymns and spiritual songs, singing with grace in your hearts to the Lord. And whatsoever ye do in word or deed, do all in the name of the Lord Jesus, giving thanks to God and the Father by him."*

Your Word will aide in us as we remain connected to You in prayer, praise, worship and in YOUR Word. You have brought us through a wilderness that held us captive by bad habits, minimal praise and worship, problems with offense, immaturity, abnormal hearing, guile in our tongue, unforgiveness of our leaders and those in authority over us. You have RELEASED us from idol worship, and You have even ministered to our appetite naturally and spiritually and we want to thank You.

You have called us to a level in You. We ask of YOU Father that YOUR fruit would remain in us. Let YOUR Word through these prayers be ENGRAFTED (carved) into our minds and hearts. Keep our appetites for prayer and the Word always on our MIND. We have matured to a place in you that we will RECOGNIZE the enemy in any form it takes, and we will guard all the entry ways giving him access (lust of the flesh, lust of the eyes, and pride of life).

Our senses will be guarded through Your Word. You've moved us from being hearers of Your Word and we thank You Father for the surgery You have performed in our hearts.

You've called the Women of Strength and Men of Valor to be INITIATORS of bowels of mercy, kindness, humbleness of mind, meekness, longsuffering, and forbearance of our sisters and brothers until they can get it together.

We are no longer quick to judge each other; we will INITIATE forgiveness and restoration. We are only able to maintain this level of Christian living as you INDWELL our hearts.

We operate in the spirit of oneness – one body having many members. No longer will we be overthrown in the wilderness by the works of the flesh or appetites of the flesh. We are not driven to the altar by pain and problems, we WANT YOU, LORD! We are frontline WORSHIP WARRIORS!

Prayer

Lord, let the Word do the work! "If you abide in Me, and My words abide in you, you will ask what you desire, and it shall be done for you" (John 15:7). I reach for Your Word to reduce any anxiety or stress. Through Your Word, I will be able to love my brother and my sister. Lord, counsel me in Your Word when I've hurt my brother or sister. I repent of any wrongdoing and I ask You to sit on the throne of my heart. Teach me, oh Lord, the way of your statutes, and I shall keep it unto the end (Psalm 119:33). From this day forward (press play), WHATEVER we do in word or deed, we do as unto the Lord. Thank You for watching over Your Word, You're a good DADDY! In Jesus' name.

Journal
The Lord's Release

Day 20

Release for Healthy Marriages

Scripture: *Mark 10:9 – "What therefore God hath joined together, let no man put asunder."*

Marriage is God's idea. It is covenant and it requires work to be healthy. A marriage is the "gym" for relationships. Marital covenant is the process of becoming ONE with another. ONE is a WHOLE number that takes an "until death do us part" timeline to become. God, in His infinite wisdom, knew that "this" covenant would bless our lives in a divine way. Marriage will unlock truths about oneself that might not otherwise be discovered. Marriage vocabulary includes words like: "our", "us", "together", "submit", "head", "love", "grow", "agreement"; did I say "submit"? And that includes submitting one to another. Love is a biggie in marriage. And not the "feely" kind of love. It's a choice! 1 Corinthians 13:4-5 says, "Love is patient, love is kind. It does not envy, it does not boast, it is not proud. It does not dishonor others, it is not self-seeking, it is not easily angered, it keeps no record of wrongs." This is the work portion of "LOVE". The enemy HATES marriage and will provide a plethora of distractions and fiery darts to "go asunder". A **distraction** is anything that takes away from your **marriage** in a way that could potentially hurt.

1. **Selfishness.** Too many of us are caught up in our own selfish wants and it diverts the attention away from our partners. Marriage is about putting our spouse first and making sure their needs are met before our own. We must remember that we are not in a relationship by ourselves; marriage is about giving more than we take.

2. **Job-Related Stress.** The stress that we allow to come home and dwell with us will eventually kill our marriage if it isn't stopped. The pressure eats away at us causing frustration and resentment that we bring home and share with our partners. It affects our communication, confidence and overall health. When we are stressed by our job, it's best to allow our spouse to support us, be that shoulder we need to lean on and that listening ear; instead of a punching bag to release on.

3. **Other people** or a grass is greener mentality. Exes on Facebook who make us feel good, a cute new friendly coworker who shows us a little bit of attention, and those not so real friends who are quick to tell us to walk away from a relationship when there is a small challenge are all major disturbances. The silver lining with this one is that we are still in control. Staying focused on the positives in our marriage leaves little room left for these other diversions.

4. **Self-Doubt and Self-Consciousness.** Being worried about things like the baby weight we're struggling to get rid of will result in our not feeling attractive or appealing to our mate. This will ultimately make us shy away from intimate experiences with our spouse. Whenever we feel inadequate, we must act. So, if its weight let's work at losing it and changing our diet. But we must keep in mind, we are as sexy as we feel, and we

must continue to do the things that make us feel good about ourselves.

5. **Money or lack of money.** Money makes people lose sight of what's most important. Many couples tend to fight over money, not be completely honest about money and have a secret "just-in-case" account which shows a lack of trust for the other partner. We cannot allow money to have dominion over our relationships. If there is less of it, we have to get creative and be honest and smart with our decisions. But love, health and joy should outweigh money any day.

Because our marriages are so fragile today, it is crucial that we remain aware of the distractions that threaten to destroy our unions. Acknowledging the challenge definitely takes some of its power away. I challenge all the couples reading this post to fight back. With a strong desire and partnership, we can overcome any of the above distractions.

Prayer

Mark 10:9 – "What therefore God hath joined together, let not man put asunder."

Dear God, I come boldly to Your throne praying for marriages everywhere, realizing two is better than one. Praying that You would bind the works of the evil one that comes to kill, steal and destroy them. Lord, I realize that marriage is an institution ordained by You. So, I pray against every evil spirit that would cause marriages to go asunder. Lord, I pray that You would deliver those that have been overtaken in sexual immorality, adultery and impurity. I pray now that You would purge marriages from every evil work – the evil works of infidelity and domestic abuse, bitterness, unforgiveness, strife and anxiety. Lord we pray now that every marriage be restored and reminded that marriage is honorable and the bed undefiled. We pray that You would send forgiveness and reconciliation to those who have walked away from their marriages. Lord, send supernatural healing, healing that only You can bring to those hearts that have been broken, and God, because of Your grace, love and the power of Your Holy Spirit we ask You to rebuild and repair marriages that have been torn down and repair the breach. Lord we now claim healing, love, peace, faithfulness, laughter and good success to every marriage and every marriage be sealed with a three-strand cord that is not easily removed. In Jesus' name. Amen.

Journal
The Lord's Release

Day 21

RELEASE FOR THE CHILDREN

Scripture: *Proverbs 22:6 – "Train them up in the way that they should go and when they are old, they won't depart from it."*

Jesus loves the little children. All the children of the world – red and yellow, black and white, they are precious in His sight. Jesus love the little children of the world. There is no other joy in being a parent – a God-given assignment to birth and parent children. You've given us the assignment to **train** them up in the way that they should go and when they are old, they won't depart from it (Proverbs 22:6). My greatest fear in parenting – what if I didn't "train" her about something that I should have taught her? The only test to know, if I did or not, was to release her into a world that I had spent so much time trying to shelter her from. I've discovered that my parenting grew as she grew. The Holy Ghost kept me abreast of things that she would never reveal, and at those times I committed it to the altar. So, Women of Strength and Men of Valor, when they don't say…just pray!!

Prayer

Proverbs 1:8-9 – "My son, hear the instruction of thy father, and forsake not the law of thy mother: For they shall be an ornament of grace unto thy head, and chains about thy neck."

Father, we come before Your presence to lift all children across the land and those unborn babies in their mother's womb. This prayer is to cover and ask for Your divine protection as the child grows from infant to adulthood. Father, we intercede for children all over because they are a heritage and they belong to You. The scripture tells us, David's heart was drawn to You at a young age. We're asking and decreeing You to draw these children's hearts to You. Let them hear You and their parent's instructions of how to live a godly and holy life. Allow them to write Your Word on the doorpost of their hearts. Teach them how to surrender to You at a young age. Keep them covered under Your divine blood. We come against the works of the enemy; whose job is to knock them off course to a road of destruction. We BIND him even now in Jesus' name. Devil, you cannot have our children. They belong to God. We will not allow you to rob them of their innocence and their future in Jesus. We come against all appetites that are not of God.

We come against drug addictions (illegal), stealing, a spirit of fornication, disobedience (to parents, teacher, etc.), spirits of bad behaviors, a spirit of harming themselves and others, youthful lusts, sexual perversion (sexual touching no penetration), a spirit of homosexuality, lying spirits (saying unkind truth about others), heavy metal music, demonic influence, sins of the mind, praying to false gods, cussing, sexual touching (no penetration), low self-esteem, rape, ungratefulness, hatred, laziness, impure thoughts, murder, selfishness, unjustified anger (attitudes), and bad grades.

Satan, by the authority of Jesus Christ, who has given me the command to bruise your head, we command you to loose your hold and take your hands from off every child in Jesus' name.

Father, I pray You cover every child across the land. We decree salvation in their lives. We call these appetites out of our children's lives in Jesus' name. Thank You for Your blood covering them. We decree they will live according to the instruction of Proverbs 1:8 and Your Word will forever be an ornament of grace unto their head and chains about their neck. In Jesus' name. Amen.

Journal
The Lord's Release

Day 22

RELEASE FOR THE NATIONS

Scripture: *Amos 3:3 – "How can two walk together, except they be agreed?"*

One nation, under God, indivisible...my Lord! How far have we drifted from this proclamation as a people? Families are dividing at a fast pace. The covenant of marriage has weakened at the core. Husbands are not loving their wives; wives are not submitting to their husbands; children are not honoring their parents; thus, we are divisible (divided). Divided families are at the core of a divisible nation. We are no longer standing under God, but rather without God. Ebenezer!!! Hitherto the Lord will help us (1 Samuel 7:12) come back under God.

Prayer

Father, in Jesus' name, we acknowledge You as creator of heaven and earth and we realize that the earth is Yours and everything in it. We pray that You would touch our nation and touch our nation's leaders. Cause us to return to (You) our first love. Lord, cause revival to break out in the land. I pray that hearts and minds will shift back to You, that as we move throughout our lives, we will never forget You; the true and living God. Lord, help us to be mindful that blessed is the nation whose God is the Lord. I pray that everyone who reads this would humble themselves, pray, seek your face and turn from their wicked ways. I ask that as we return from the darkness of this evil world to the light of Your dear son that You would cause healing to take place in the land and forgive the sins of the nation. Lord, because of this prayer we believe You now that the nation is receiving a heart of repentance, that we are returning to You, our first love. Thank You that our nation is returning to You just as the prodigal son returned home. Thank You for a reconciled nation. In Jesus' name. Amen.

Journal
The Lord's Release

Day 23

Release Among Pastors

Scripture: *Philippians 2:3-4 – "Do nothing out of selfish ambition or vain conceit. Rather, in humility value others above yourselves, not looking to your own interests but each of you to the interests of the others."*

Revelation 2:23 – "And I will kill her children with death; and all the churches shall know that I am he which searcheth the reins and hearts: and I will give unto every one of you according to your works."

This Delilah is not a person, it's the spirit operating through Delilah. This spirt of Delilah uses every means of sexual perversion known in hell to seduce the men and women of God. This spirit wants to corrupt these men and women of God. Stop letting the devil come between you and God, stop allowing him to break up families, etc. He has given His pastors space to repent and they repented not. The spirit of Delilah is an anointing killer, it's out to destroy your ministry, family and your reputation. The enemy has released a seducing called lust, men and women of God. It's time to take up your spiritual weapon and fight.

Don't be fooled by the tactics of this spirit. I hear the Lord say, do not YIELD to temptation. Men and women of God, pull out your secret weapons and fight. This fight will not be won in the natural, I have given you POWER to tread on the serpent and to bruise his head.

Father, we come to invade the enemy's territory and dismantle his kingdom. We come to snatch back our pastors, godly men and women of God. The enemy is wreaking habit in ministries and causing our men and women to fall from grace. We come against every lust and sexual demon and are asking You, Father, to kill every strange spirit that is causing these men and women to fall in temptation. We cover every entrance where the enemy will cause them to fall, we cover their eyes (keep their eyes on God and in the Word), ears (they are to hear Your voice, mouth (speak of the goodness of the Lord), heart (seeking after the heart of God), mind (guard their thinking), hands (not to touch any unclean things) and feet (stay on the straight and narrow road) under Your precious blood in Jesus' name. We put every body part on the altar for Your godly alteration. You told them to resist the devil and he will flee. Too many of them are yielding to temptation and giving into their fleshly, sexual appetites. We BIND that stronghold off our men and women of God. We serve notice on the enemy. God is rescuing his pastors from your clutches. You can no longer tempt these godly men and women in Jesus' name. As we intercede for pastors, we pray You be the center of each pastor's heart, keep them humble before You, let them be godly men and women before You and in the ministry.

According to 1 Timothy 2:2, "...all who are in authority, that we may lead a quiet and peaceable life in all godliness and reverence." In these evil times, You are looking for holy, godly, righteous and humble men and women of God.

What to look for:

- Men/women searching the person out (scavenger hunt, he's going to and fro seeking God's anointed)
- He/she doesn't love me
- He/she doesn't give me sex like he/she used to

- Just this one time, no one will know (God will know)
- Every pastor is sleeping around (the devil is a liar)
- Meet me after church
- Him – what type of underwear do you have on
- My wife doesn't dress sexy for me
- He/she is inquiring of what perfume/cologne you're wearing
- He/she gave me a hug… (hands share to wonder)
- He/she wants to control their fleshly appetite with the power of sexual passion for the purpose of possessing these men and women of God
- Women exposing their body
- Tight dresses/shirts
- Low cut tops
- Short dresses/skirts
- Flirting spirit (eyes and mouth)
- Entrance of the eye (eyes will capture a seductive glance)
- He/she is whispering in the ear

Prayer

Father, we intercede on the behalf of every pastor. We ask You to fill their lives with Your presence, power and a double portion of Your anointing. We go after the root of these symptoms and cast it back into the pit. You said You will not leave us nor forsake us. Thank You that the spirit of the Lord is upon Pastor_____. There is an anointing that is on his/her life. Satan, I command you to take your hands off these men and women of God in Jesus' name. Thank You for gifting my Pastor_____ with Your wisdom, knowledge and understanding as he/she stands behind the sacred desk to decree and declare Your Word. Continue to allow my Pastor_____ to walk in the spirit of Your righteousness and holiness. Teach him/her how to go in and out and keep him/her covered under Your blood. Father, keep Your hand upon my pastor, keep him/her prayed up and strong in the Word of God. Keep my pastor from falling into the clutches of the devil's devices of pride, greed, sexual desire outside his/her marriage, adultery, fornication and the spirit of deception in Jesus' name. We grab hold to 2 Corinthians 10:4, "For the weapons of our warfare are not carnal, but mighty through God to the pulling down of the strong holds." We pull them down in Jesus' name. Amen.

Journal
The Lord's Release

Day 24

RELEASE AMONG PASTOR'S WIVES

Scripture: *Genesis 2:18 – "And the Lord God said, it is not good that the man should be alone. I will make him a help meet for him."*

Who called her? The Pastor's wife, she is called to be an indispensable companion and HELPER to her husband. Her role, ever changing based on the strengths and needs of her husband's "calling". A role solely birthed from a call of her husband and that can go away just as fast. She is ever earning her place not as his wife but as the "help meet" – companion. The blueprint for a "good" pastor's wife is subjective to the needs of the pastor/husband and the congregation. The role is ever changing and evolving. Often encouraged to "be yourself" but that mostly doesn't work, so we must remain moldable and pliable. Don't work to be a "good" pastor's wife but strive to please little 'L' so that his heart will safely trust in you (Proverbs 31:11). Much prayer is needed for her. She must balance home and church, different personalities, wavering wants and needs, unspoken rules, silent heartaches, yet remain publicly together. She needs strength to have spiritual impact in the ministry and among the people.

Prayer

Dear Heavenly Father, we thank You for pastors' wives everywhere. Thank You for the love, strength and faithfulness they exhibit to their husbands and others. I pray now that You would continue to strengthen them for the journey and grant them grace and peace for the years ahead. Let them know that they are never alone. You will hear them when they pray. Lord, when they feel weak, please wrap your loving arms around them reminding them not to fear but be strong and courageous. You will never leave them nor forsake them (Deuteronomy 31:6). Lord, when they grow tired and weary You will cause them to be renewed and soar as eagles (Isaiah 40:31). Father, may they never look outside of You for comfort, but let them know You are a comforter and a keeper; You are their hope and peace. I pray that they walk not after the flesh but after the spirit; that You would guide them into all truth. I pray that every plan of the enemy be canceled now in Jesus' name. We cancel the spirit of lack, misunderstandings, selfishness, lack of concern, resentment, laziness and lack of communication. Now God, cause them to increase in Your power and beauty and in grace, cause them to always be a figure of love, understanding, strength, faithfulness and hope. Bless them as they walk in righteousness and keep Your light shining bright for all who will follow. Amen.

Journal
The Lord's Release

Day 25

RELEASE OF INTERCESSORS

Scripture: *2 Corinthians 10:3-5 – "For though we walk in the flesh, we do not war after the flesh: For the weapons of our warfare are not carnal, but mighty through God to the pulling down of strong holds; Casting down imaginations, and every high thing that exalteth itself against the knowledge of God, and bringing into captivity every thought to the obedience of Christ."*

Intercession is prayer that pleads with God for my needs and the needs of others. But it is also much more than that. Intercession involves taking hold of God's WILL and refusing to let go until HIS WILL comes to pass.

A family member faces a deadly disease. Your neighbor desperately needs Jesus but turns away every time you try to share Christ. A nation begins to crumble because its people follow their own evil ways. But what can you do?

Often, the problems we face seem too big for us. No matter how much we try, we cannot solve them on our own. It's times like these when we need to turn to the Lord in intercessory prayer.

Intercession is warfare -- the key to God's battle plan for our lives. But the battleground is not of this earth. The Bible says we are not fighting against flesh and blood. We are fighting against forces and authorities and against rulers of darkness and spiritual powers in the heavens above (Ephesians 6:12). Intercessory prayer takes place in this spiritual world where the battles for our own lives, our families, our friends and our nation are won or lost.

Jesus is in control of the situation. Jesus "rules over forces, authorities, powers, and rulers ... over all beings in this world and will rule in the future world as well" (Ephesians 1:21). He is King of Kings and Lord of Lords. Ephesians 6 teaches us to be ready to fight with God's weapons. These are the "weapons of our warfare" that can pull down strongholds in the spirit world (2 Corinthians 10:3-4). They will also protect you from the attacks that are sure to come once you begin the spiritual battle. We must bind the work of Satan, knowing that Jesus has given you authority "to defeat the power of your enemy" (Luke 10:19).

If God shows you the identity of specific spiritual strongholds that are at work, take authority over these strongholds in the name of Jesus. And always remember that "God's Spirit is in you and is more powerful than the one that is in the world" (1 John 4:4).

Finally, as you begin the spiritual battle, take comfort knowing that you are not alone; Jesus is also interceding on your behalf! The Bible says that Jesus is able to save forever those who draw near to God through Him, since He always lives to make intercession for them (Hebrews 7:25, Romans 8:26-27, 34).

Intercessors don't give up. We endure all setbacks and overcome every obstacle. We take hold to the horns of the altar with prayers that "press on" until we "apprehend" God's will in whatever situation we are facing. (Philippians 3:12). Intercessors know that prayer is the key to seeing breakthroughs in your life and in the lives of those around you.

Prayer

Lord God, we pray for the awakening of every intercessor. Let them not be weary in well doing for in due season they will reap if they faint not. Lord, Your Word says men should always pray and faint not. We pray for those that operate in the ministry of intercession to be reminded by way of Your spirit to build up the Body of Christ daily. To build up a wall of protection around Your people from the enemy. To create hedges of protection and remove barriers from those that are blocked. To be reminded that we're fighting for justice on behalf of another that is weak and being called to the ministry. There is an anointing to make things move in the realm of the spirit. Proverbs 24:10 says if we faint in the day of adversity our strength is small. Build up every intercessor, Lord. Build up their understanding, give them a knowing that a work is being done; therefore, the enemy will try to make sure it's not done. We must submit ourselves to God in prayer; we must keep praying. Intercession for our families, as well as others. Remind them that God looks for our intercessions. In Ezekiel 22:30, God looked for someone who would build up the wall and stand before Him in the gap on behalf of the land, so He wouldn't have to destroy it. Thank You for the awakening of Your intercessors to rise up in prayer night and day. I thank You that Your word says the angels hearken to the Word of the Lord. May Your angels go forth now as You have commanded them charge over us, to arise every intercessor in the four corners of the earth on today. In the mighty name of Jesus, I pray, Amen.

Journal
The Lord's Release

Day 26

Release from Generational Curses

Scripture: *Exodus 34:7 – "Keeping mercy for thousands, forgiving iniquity and transgression and sin, and that will by no means clear the guilty; visiting the iniquity of the fathers upon the children, and upon. The children's children, unto the third and to the fourth generation."*

A generational curse is believed to be passed down from one generation to another due to rebellion against God. This belief comes from Old Testament passages which say that God "punishes the children and their children for the sins of the fathers to the third and fourth generation". Psalm 51:5 says, "Behold, I was shapen in iniquity; and in sin did my mother conceive me."

When the umbilical cord was cut, the **transfer stopped**! Ezekiel 18:20 says, "The soul that sinneth, it shall die. The son shall not bear the iniquity of the father, neither shall the father bear the iniquity of the son: the righteousness of the righteous she be upon him, and the wickedness of the wicked shall be upon him." Hallelujah! It stops with me. Glory! I open up the umbrella of grace, mercy and His word over MY head in every matter that has been consistent in my family line. I have my own sins to confess and be free, no time to deal with a bad inheritance…

Jesus! Behavioral traits and habits from family can be cancelled out but I stand firm that I WILL not operate and function under a CURSE! God has redeemed us from the curses being passed on from one generation to the next. This redemption comes as we understand that the root of our problems is in the spiritual realm. Women of Strength and Men of Valor, apply God's Word and power to your lives and choose to walk in righteousness and obedience to God, the chains of bondage will be broken!

Prayer

Father in Jesus' name, as I pray, I stand firm on Your Word in John 8:36, "If the son therefore shall make you free, you shall be free indeed." I declare that, according to Galatians 3:13, I have been redeemed from the curse of the law, by the sacrifice of Jesus. So right now, I rebuke and renounce every curse in my bloodline, and I ask You to cleanse me in Your blood. I pray now for freedom and victory over every generational curse, the curse of disease, of poverty and lack, of depression and anxiety, of mental health and suicide, of anger and bitterness, of envy and murder, of jealousy and hatred, of sexual immorality and broken marriages, of rejection and abandonment. I pray now, in Jesus' name, that You would loose the bands of wickedness and undo the heavy burdens, to let the oppressed go free. I decree and declare that I am free today from the sins of our fathers and every evil work. For sin shall not be my master because I am now not under the law, but under grace (Romans 6:14). For in Christ Jesus the law of the spirit of life has set me free from the law of death. Amen.

Journal
The Lord's Release

Day 27

Release from Infirmities

Scripture: *Hebrews 4:16 – "Let us therefore come boldly unto the throne of grace, that we may obtain mercy, and find grace to help in time of need."*

Father, Your words tell us we can come boldly unto the throne of grace in time of need for healing in our physical body. You said in Your Word, according to 3 John 2:2, that You wish we would be in good health, even as our soul prospereth. We take to heart this scripture as we come against those infirmities that have been attacking our bodies.

Father in Jesus' name, we pray that You keep our bodies free of disease. Touch those that have been afflicted by illness or an attack of the enemy, heal them and cause them to recover. Lord, You are the one that healeth the broken hearted and binds up their wounds. So, we pray that You would heal according to Your will. Then God, help us to realize that our bodies are not our own. We are the temple of the Holy Spirit. Teach us to number our days that we may apply our hearts to wisdom. Help us begin to practice healthy and righteous living. I pray that we prosper and enjoy good health even as our souls prosper. I pray now against every would be distractive, destructive spirit, the spirit of mental illness, emotional struggles, feelings of hopelessness and abandonment, and the spirit of suicide and loneliness. Lord, help us to focus our minds on You that we may be kept in perfect peace, Your peace that passes all understanding that will keep our hearts and minds through Christ Jesus.

Prayer

Father, we come boldly to you. I come first asking You to forgive me from my sins and to cleanse me from all unrighteousness in Jesus' name. As I come before Your presence, I am at fault for this door being open, I repent before You and heaven and confess this sin and ask You to cleanse me and shut this door in Jesus' name. Forgive me for the infirmity of past hurt, when I hurt others, of those who offended me, when I offended them, when I was bitter against my sisters and brothers, and when they were bitter against me.

Father, You said in Your Word that You would heal us of all our sickness and disease. I come to tread on every infirmity of sickness and disease in Jesus' name. I take authority over these infirmities. I need a healing in Jesus' name. John 14:14 says, "If you ask anything in My name, I will do it." Since You said I can come boldly and ask, I'm asking you to heal Your people of their infirmities. So, I bind the tactics of Satan and his demonic spirits of infirmity in Jesus' name. I come against every attack from the enemy and grab hold to Your healing virtue in Jesus' name.

Father, I release these infirmities from Your people at their root and send them back to the pit of hell in Jesus' name: Cancer (all types including blood), Anxiety, Epilepsy, Congestive Heart Failure, Flu, Eye Disease, Chronic Pain, Asthma, Fever in children, Allergies, ADHD, Fibroids, Alzheimer's, High Blood Pressure, Fibromyalgia, Arthritis, Binge Eating, Wheelchair Bound, Bipolar Disorder, Brain Tumors, Hearing Loss, Bronchitis, Bulimia, Sex Trafficking (Illness), Chest Pain, High Cholesterol, TB, Mental Illness, Insomnia, Leg Cramps, Blindness, Miscarriage, Lupus, Abscess, Migraine, Depression, Diabetes, Thymus Gland/Myasthenia Gravis, Obesity, Earache (deafness), Sleep Apnea, Parkinson's Disease, Pneumonia, Sickle Cell, Suicide, Leukemia, Vertigo and Stroke.

Father, we pray in the name of Jesus that every sickness and disease is under the blood in Jesus' name. We curse the root of these diseases and cancel every assignment of the enemy in Jesus' name. Father, I cast all these diseases at the feet of Jesus for Him to heal Your people. As I decree these healings, I seal these healings in Your name, Jehovah Rapha. Father, we acknowledge You as our ultimate healer from every infirmity.

Journal
The Lord's Release

Day 28

RELEASE FROM THE SPIRT OF OFFENSE

Scripture: *Luke 17:1* – "Then said he unto the disciples, It is impossible but that offences will come: but woe *unto him*, through whom they come!"

Offense is a bait of Satan! It lures us into longstanding, broken relationships. Offense is a deadly weapon that kills relationships and builds up bitterness. It is tied to pride and control. Offense means 1) A breach of a law or rule, an illegal act or 2) Annoyance or resentment brought about by a PERCEIVED insult to or disregard for oneself or one's standards or principles. I'm highlighting PERCEIVED because a lot of time the offender might not know that they have offended you. The enemy makes it look like they are walking around acting like they haven't done anything, and for some, they don't know that they did anything. Unless properly identified, and repentance and change come forth, the spirit of offense will continue to cause chaos and destroy relationships.

The spirit of offense has infiltrated our relationships and causes division, dissension, strife, hurt and pain. Women of Strength and Men of Valor, the Bible tells us "Be sober, be vigilant; because your adversary the devil, as a roaring lion, walketh about, seeking whom he may devour" (1 Peter

5:8). We must ask for a discerning spirit so that we can move beyond "faces" and discern the spirit behind the words, the offense. Too many wasted years, months, days, hours, minutes and seconds lost because of offense. Offense is like quicksand. What **can** make **quicksand** deadly is its ability to trap and hold unsuspecting victims (saints). God wants us free. Matthew 18:7 tells us, "Woe unto the world because of offences! for it must needs be that offences come; but woe to that man by whom the offence cometh!" We must be intentional to fight against the spirit of offense. We cast off every characteristic of offense. When we walk in offense, we feel a sense of:

Entitlement – The person with offense feels they are owed something. They value what they have in themselves and feel they have worked hard, and they deserve to be elevated or recognized. The truth is they felt they deserved something they weren't entitled to. Entitled people feel it is their duty and responsibility even though it isn't. When they feel entitled to a position or thing and don't receive it, they get offended and rejected.

Pride – Prideful people are self-reliant instead of God-reliant. When pride attacks, it doesn't allow us to see the "big" picture. Lucifer was prideful and it resulted in his fall. When people are offended, the offense is rooted in pride. Pride makes us fall; however, with offense people don't see the fall as a result of their own doing, but they put the blame on others. Some people cannot handle the thought of being wrong and then they feel shameful and unworthy. When a person offers direction or correction to a prideful, offensive person, often it is interpreted as I can't do anything right or I messed up again.

Unfairness – People with offense often feel church leaders (i.e. pastors or pastors' wives) have treated them unfairly. The one offended says *"they didn't value my gifting; they pay attention to everyone else but not* *me"*. People get hurt and build up resentment and bitterness when they are not used in the church or they think attention is given to one more than the other. What people don't realize is that there is proper order in a healthy church or relationship.

Respect – The world has taught us to demand respect, but the Bible has taught us to humble ourselves and serve with love. When offended, what the world has taught us screams in our ears and we cannot hear the quietness of the Lord's voice that says serve with humility.

Control – Offensive people often desire to control the situation. When control and having it my way cannot exist, offensive people get offended and leave the church or relationship. If only they would have stayed under the strong leadership that didn't put up with their selfish behaviors, they may have received the healing they were longing for but didn't know they needed.

There are pastors and leaders who will put up with offensive people in an attempt to usher them into deliverance and manifest the giftings within them. Unfortunately, offensive people think everyone else is wrong and they are the only one who is right. Therefore, when a genuine person comes into their life or is sent by God, they often don't receive them because they don't know how to receive unconditional love, correction and instruction.

People with offense become unteachable in their pursuit to be elevated, entitled and respected. They can't receive the fact that this situation or church will be different from the last encounter. They are still elevating themselves and can't believe that someone may have more knowledge or growth in their spiritual walk. They often would rather be argumentative than pursue peace and humility.

Women of Strength and Men of Valor, "Submit yourselves therefore to God. Resist the devil, and he will flee from you" (James 4:7).

Prayer

Philippians 2:5 – "Let this mind be in you which was also in Christ Jesus."

Father, help us to establish "healthy boundaries" through Your Word. Father, our mind! We need You to get in our mind – the way we think, how we process information in our mind as it relates to offense. Keep our mind healthy and sharp on a daily basis. Allow us daily to have the mind of Christ Jesus. Keep us from thinking negative when offense rises to the surface. You said You will keep us in perfect peace if we keep our mind on You. Father, help us to identify offense when it comes and help us to be slow to anger. We pray that when the spirit of offense comes, we're able to release forgiveness immediately. Offense is a spirit that causes chaos, pain, hurt, strife, discord, control and pride; it allows us to become unteachable and wreaks havoc in one's life. We come against the spirit of offense and cast it on the altar. Father, offense can destroy relationships whether in marriages, families or colleagues, and causes division in churches.

Father, we come to BIND the spirit of offense and release in the atmosphere a spirit of forgiveness and to love them according to Your Word. Even while Jesus was on the cross, He spoke into the atmosphere in Luke 23:34, "Father, forgive them, for they do not know what they do." He goes to tell us to lay aside every weight and sin that easily beset us. Let us not operate in a negative spirit when offense comes. Amen.

Journal
The Lord's Release

Day 29

Release from Adultery

Scripture: *Exodus 20:14 "Thou shalt not commit adultery - This commandment forbids all acts of uncleanness, with all those desires, which produce those acts and war against the soul."*

Adultery made the list! We have become desensitized to this spirit that has crept into the church. My heart breaks for the number of reports that a pastor, pastor's wife, or leaders in the church have fallen victim to this spirit! I get it in the world where there are no rules but, in the church, we are taught to deal with our flesh! Galatians 5:16 says, "This I say then, walk in the Spirit, and ye shall not fulfil the lust of the flesh." I'm burdened that we have lost respect of the Word of God and each other. Infidelity, cheating, inappropriate conversations, infatuation, flirting, fondling, explicit pictures or text messages, etc., messes with the VOW! Ecclesiastes 5: 4-6 says, "When thou vowest a vow unto God, defer not to pay it; for he hath no pleasure in fools: pay that which thou hast vowed. Better is it that thou shouldest not vow, than that thou shouldest vow and not pay. Suffer not thy mouth to cause thy flesh to sin; neither say thou before the angel, that it was an error: wherefore should God be angry at thy voice, and destroy the work of thine hands?"

With tears flowing, I'm extremely saddened that this offense is commonly reported among pastors and their wives. We are not exempt from the devil's devices. Forming emotional ties, couched under "work", "meetings", and "counseling", that brings questions or discomfort should be considered. And the thought that it happened with someone we know, had close fellowship with, spent time with, shared special moments with is an unbearable heartbreak. Adultery is not a matter just between two people; so many are hurt by it. It is as hurtful as murder, and the devastating effects never go away entirely. The offenders had the privilege of making the choice to engage in adultery, but families have no choice about the suffering inflicted upon them. It messes with the VOW! And the price you pay for submitting to adultery is more than the cost of any lavish wedding.

Prayer

Dear God, help us walk in remembrance of the great sacrifice that was made to purchase our salvation on Calvary. I pray we realize that our bodies are not our own, we were purchased with the precious blood of Jesus. Help us honor our temple and not defile it through the working of sinful flesh. God, we ask You to free the mind and destroy yokes. We ask You to send deliverance to any that would walk in or seek to walk in adultery, sexual immorality, perversion, impurity or debauchery and cause them to flee youthful lust and pursue righteousness, faith, love and peace with those who call on the Lord out of a pure heart. Lord, we take authority over the enemy of the body, soul and mind, we cast down every stronghold that comes to destroy.

We command Satan to put down his weapons and flee, God has given us authority and power to tread upon serpents and scorpions and over all the power of the enemy. So, we command the spirit of adultery to be cast out of hearts and minds. We bind every evil, would be perverted thought in Jesus' name. We command minds to be free, every soul tie be destroyed, and hearts cleansed from inordinate affections. We pray that transformation takes place with the renewing of the mind and let our minds be transformed to the mind of Christ Jesus. Amen.

Journal
The Lord's Release

Day 30

THIS IS THE LORD'S RELEASE

Scripture: *Deuteronomy 15:2b. – "Because it is called the Lord's release…"*

At the end of every seven years though shalt make a release (Deuteronomy 15: 1). We waste so much time holding on to things that we should simply RELEASE! The Bible is clear of laws regarding RELEASE; laws regarding releasing the poor from debts, releasing slaves and the free or being released to be a blessing. The Lord's release is a FULL release. That means one is not just making a payment but paid in full! No more obligation to whatever is owed. The release brought honor and glory to God. Sin debts are blotted out by the blood of the Lamb.

Forgiveness is an area that most struggle with because we believe that there should be some repayment/vengeance for being wronged. Selective or partial forgiveness is not forgiveness. Galatians 5:9 says, "A little Leaven leaveneth the whole lump." Sickness and disease are trapped in bodies because of unforgiveness. The "WHO" or "WHAT" doesn't justify the indebtedness. Feelings are not a substitute of entitlement to stay in debt to whatever your "IT" is. This is the Lord's release! BE healed, BE delivered, BE set free!

Prayer

Father, this is not an all-inclusive list but for the areas identified in this daily journal, I pray that You will lead me to areas to pray over. Not just one day but any day that I need strength as I encounter a specific area. These prayers are spirit led, inspired and prayed starting in 2007. The move of Your Spirit to pray about the areas identified in this book are to bring a breaking of chains, deliverance, challenge to change, conviction and repentance. Be glorified in the praying of these prayers. Release me from any area that has kept me bound in Jesus' name. "So shall my word be that goeth forth out of my mouth: it shall not return unto me void, but it shall accomplish that which I please, and it shall prosper in the thing whereto I sent it" (Isaiah 55:11). I declare and decree, I am free according to the word that I have prayed in this book. I've overcome by the word of my testimony that I have written in this journal. Thank you, Lord, that every soul tie, boundary, curse, past issue, and sleeping giant's power is broken off of my life. In Jesus' name. Amen.

Journal
The Lord's Release

www.ingramcontent.com/pod-product-compliance
Lightning Source LLC
Chambersburg PA
CBHW021114080526
44587CB00010B/521